BRAND YOU

BECOME THE EXPERT

A STEP-BY-STEP GUIDE TO BUILDING

YOUR PERSONAL UNIQUE BRAND™

FOR MORE SALES, MORE CLIENTS, MORE OFTEN

LISA LIEBERMAN-WANG & WILLARD BARTH

CONTACT

To Book Lisa or Willard for Corporate Events

Call 1-877-250-7275

www.BrandYouBecomeTheExpert

BRAND YOU BECOME THE EXPERT
ISBN: 9781651909263

This book is dedicated to you, our reader, for your desire to move forward and become a better you, to share your gifts with the world.

This book is also dedicated to the thousands of individuals around the globe who have joined the never-ending journey of personal development and entrepreneurship in order to achieve your dreams.

Your continuous dedication to improving yourself and making a difference has inspired us to be our best. It is because of you that this book is possible. Empowering and inspiring others to share their unsaid and unheard truth is what makes us real and enables us to make a difference.

Finally, this book is dedicated to our family and friends who continue to support us every step of the way!

Table of Contents

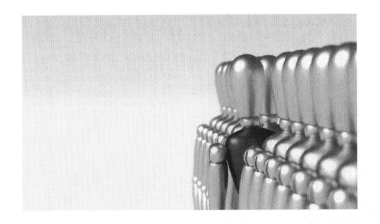

Introduction

You have a choice in today's economy. You are the elite, superlative product or service of choice; a commodity, which is a mass-produced, unspecialized product; or a discount provider.

Most businesses are competing in the commodity space. Everyone is trying to get your attention by screaming, but is anyone speaking your language to what you really care about? The average business does not understand the psychology of their customers.

Businesses suffer from "Marketing Myopia" "focusing on products rather than customer" according to Theodore Levitt.

The paradigm needs to shift today to being more focused on your customers' needs and wants and how you can fill it.

This creates a unique question, "What business are you REALLY in?" This process will help you understand that what you think your business has been is not the core of what your business should be.

Making yourself stand out from the competition in a noisy marketplace can be challenging but not impossible.

To position yourself in the elite category you need to know two things. 1) Who you are, and 2) Who *specifically* is your ideal client. Then brand yourself to be the leader serving your ideal client's needs.

Only when your ideal client knows that you understand their biggest problem and are the expert with the best solution to solve that problem will they be ready to do business with you. And if you can demonstrate that you are the expert in your field and deliver the most value, then you are no longer "competing" on price but able to charge based on the value you deliver.

The challenge is how do you brand yourself so your clients can find you?

We hear about it all the time on the internet, people coming out of nowhere and becoming an apparently overnight success. What you don't see is the strategy and blueprint that got them there. We will give you proven strategy and tactics that we have personally used and helped our clients implement to generate six and seven figures in their businesses with some of them starting from nothing.

Brand You Become the Expert is the starting point, giving you insights into the mindset, strategies and resources that can take your business and elevate it to the elite status where you determine and set the industry standard.

Lisa Lieberman-Wang & Willard Barth
#1 International Best-Selling Authors
Co-Founders NAP Leadership & Coaching Academy™
Co-Creators NAP, Neuro Associative Programming™

You know what a brand is. Apple, Tesla, Lexus, McDonald's, Levi's, Band-Aid, and Rolex are all brands.

But do you know what a Personal Unique Brand™ is? And, even more important, do you know how to build one?

If you answered, "No," to either of those questions, then this book is for you.

Today, you need a Personal Unique Brand™ more than ever. If you want to stand out from the competition, attract new customers and build a successful company, building a Personal Unique Brand™ is crucial.

If you're an entrepreneur, investing at least some time each week to improve your brand is important. As you will learn later, one of your greatest assets in your business is your Personal Unique Brand™.

Your Personal Unique Brand™ can take your business to places you never thought possible.

But you must know how to build one.

Sadly, most business owners are unable to create a Personal Unique Brand™. They have no clear direction on exactly what steps to take and what's involved in creating a brand around themselves. That's what this book is all about.

We're going to give you a blueprint that will walk you through:

❖ What is a Personal Unique Brand™?
❖ Why you need a Personal Unique Brand™
❖ A step-by-step guide to building your own Personal Unique Brand™

Ready?
Let's dive in.

BRAND YOU

Chapter 1

What Is a Personal Unique Brand™?

The "Brand You" concept has existed for some time now, and we are standing on the shoulders of giants in the marketing and business world. Now, we are taking "Brand You" to the next level. We're exponentially expanding on the Brand You concept; creating a new operating system by which you can achieve and reap the results of tapping into the persuasive power of Brand You through YOUR own **Personal Unique Brand™**. Now we are leveraging our expertise in neuroscience, human psychology, marketing, advertising and decades of success in personal and professional transformation to turn the original Brand You concept into an explosive business model and bio-hack for exponential growth.

A Personal Unique Brand™ is more than just a bold logo or a choice of specific colors. A Personal Unique Brand™ goes much further than having a business card that looks nice. It's not about just getting a website with your name on it, but that's certainly part of it.

A Personal Unique Brand™ is much bigger and all-encompassing. It's about who you are and what you do.

Your Personal Unique Brand™ is how you present yourself, both online, offline and in every interaction with your ideal client.

The image you put forth is your Personal Unique Brand™. That's what you're communicating. The values you live by. The essence of who you really are as a person. Your Personal Unique Brand™ is your secret sauce that distinguishes you from all the others. It's what's specific to you.

Your Personal Unique Brand™ includes your:

- ❖ Values
- ❖ Unique skills
- ❖ Experiences
- ❖ Stories
- ❖ Personality
- ❖ Image

And each of these must be presented in an authentic, honest way to your audience.

Ultimately, your Personal Unique Brand™ is built around you. It's about what you're offering, the benefit you're bringing to the table. This includes the specific ways you can overcome the deepest points of frustration and the biggest problems of your ideal client.

You may be tempted to think that only big companies are brands, but that's not true. Thanks to the internet and the power of social media, every person can be their own brand.

- ❖ Everyone can constantly put themselves out in front of their audience.
- ❖ Everyone can add value to their audience.
- ❖ Everyone can communicate their message loud and clear.

We all have the tools to build powerful Personal Unique Brands™.

In fact, you might say that every person is already a brand. The question is whether you are actively taking control of your brand.

Here's the reality: You can ignore your Personal Unique Brand™ and let it develop based on people's perceptions, which are often incorrect and possibly destructive to your brand, leaving it out of your control, or you can help manage your Personal Unique Brand™ to position yourself as the person you want to be.

Whether you like it or not, you have a Personal Unique Brand™. Anything you share online, every email you send to your audience, every blog you write, every live event you host -- it's all part of your brand.

Each and every contact point shapes the way people think about you and the image your put forth.
The question is whether you want your brand to evolve on its own, without any input from you, or

whether you want to be directly in control of the process.

Clearly, it is better to guide our potential client to the perspective and call-to-action we prefer than to leave that critical thought process to chance.

So how do you build a Personal Unique Brand™ proactively? How do you get the development of it under your control? How do you help build your reputation with your brand?

That's what the rest of this book is about.

Chapter 2

Why You Need To Brand

You?

You might think at this point, "Why do I need to establish a Personal Unique Brand™?" I'm not a big business. I'm not a famous entertainer or athlete. Why should I worry about a brand?

Here's the reality: Every entrepreneur, speaker, coach, consultant, freelancer, etc. should be building their own brand.

It doesn't matter if you're not a famous person or a Fortune 500 company.

It's important to build your own Personal Unique Brand™ if you're going to build a company of any kind.

Let's discuss some of the rewards of creating a Personal Unique Brand™.

Personal Unique Branding™
Allows You to Stand Out from the
Competition

First and foremost, building a Personal Unique Brand™ enables you to stand out from your competition.

Your brand, values, expertise, and story all set you apart from your competitors.

Your competitors can't bring what you bring to the table.

They simply don't have what you have to offer. You're unique. Only you are you.

You have unique:

- ❖ Experiences
- ❖ Strengths
- ❖ Beliefs
- ❖ Perspectives
- ❖ Skills
- ❖ Insights

...that set you apart from everyone else. These are incredibly valuable and distinguish you from your competitors.

You are offering a unique value that no one else can offer. Nobody else can bring what you can to the table. No one else has a unique set of skills, knowledge and experiences. This is your *confidence formula* and the key to creating your own intellectual property.

Building your Personal Unique Brand™ allows you to highlight your uniqueness.

It allows you to take full advantage of your strengths. Which enables the best parts of you to be revealed. It sets you apart from all your rivals. All of this gives you a significant competitive advantage.

Think about Rolex and how they separated themselves from the competition. When they focused exclusively on being a luxury watch manufacturer, they set the standard above all other watch makers.

For those who want a luxury watch, Rolex is *the* brand, while Timex is the brand for those who want a durable, relatively low-cost watch.

The more you work to build your Personal Unique Brand™, the greater edge you'll have over your competition. You'll stand out amongst the crowd.

Personal Unique Branding™

Allows You to Charge a

Premium Price

As noted, Personal Unique Branding™ highlights just how exceptional you are and the incredible value that you offer.

You can charge a premium price for your services since you bring unique value to the marketplace-- value that no one else provides. You shouldn't be exchanging time for money anymore; you're delivering significant value and need to be rewarded for it.

After all, you provide something they can't find elsewhere; only you are delivering your unique services.

Remember, when you craft a strong Personal Unique Brand™, you can charge a higher price for your products and services because they're exclusive to you. They can't be purchased at another store or from another person.

As your brand becomes stronger, more people want your services. As more customers want your services, the higher the price you can charge.

That's exactly why Nike can charge so much for their shoes. They've been developing their brand into a powerhouse for years. Nike shoes have become a sign of wealth, and wearing Nikes shows the world who you are.

This enables Nike to sell their shoes for exorbitant amounts of money. In the customer's mind, the Nike brand immediately equates to higher quality and higher shoe prices.

Follow their example and you can also charge a premium price. Work hard to build your Personal Unique Brand™ and demonstrate how much value you bring to the table.

This can apply in any profession. Here are three perfect examples from our clients including one who is a naturopathic physician.

"As a Health Professional, One of the Single BEST INVESTMENTS I ever made in myself and my practice was working with Lisa & Willard."

I stopped undervaluing my services and implemented the tools from their program.

For 15 years my initial consultation would cost my patients $399 of which only $66 was profit. I immediately applied all they taught me, and I was able to brand myself, creating a new unique value *proposition which became a three-month program. We created my Personal Unique Brand™ and my first package sold was $3,500. I "just did it".*

In less than 10 days I increased my prices and generated over $21,000. By the end of the first month I had earned over $45,000. My income has increased by 1000%. The programs they offer are PRICELESS! I have registered for every one of them."

I am working even smarter, not harder and my patients are getting extraordinary results as it pays to pay attention. I now have a waiting list for my services."

Dr. Terry White

Natural Balance Concepts LLC, Naturopathic Doctor, Certified NAP/NLP Practitioner

"I'm a single mom of two beautiful children. I have been in business for several years but was having a hard time charging more for my services and communicating my packages.

Lisa helped me change my marketing to attract more clients with my Personal Unique Brand™. I moved from promoting what my clients were doing with me to what they would be getting from working with me. Then we got clear on identifying my ideal client. With just a few small tweaks, in *just 3 days of applying what I learned I got 3 new VIP clients bringing in an additional $9000."*

Melanie Moore, UK

Big Vision Coach & Host Big Vision TV

"I have made 1200% more money this year than I had in my own business of 15 years because I followed what I have learned from working with Lisa & Willard!

We created my own Personal Unique Brand™ combining all my experience from my education becoming a Certified Neuro Associative Programming (NAP) & Neuro Linguist Programming (NLP) Practitioner, learning neuroscience and human psychology, along with my energy work in becoming a Reiki Master. Then trademarked my services as Transformative Neuro-Reiki™.

This year I earned part-time over $94,000 working 20 hours a week. Plus...One day I made $17,000 from an event with less than a dozen people. I remember a time I didn't make that in a year. Now, I'm on track for six figures part time. Much Love!"

Brenda Kiss

BKiss, Certified NAP & NLP Practitioner & Transformative Neuro-Reiki™ Master

Personal Unique Branding™

Highlights Your Expertise

Remember, your Personal Unique Brand™ is how you present yourself to the world.

It is important that the information you share with the world contains a significant amount of Personal Unique Branding™.

The more valuable the content you share, the more you convey that you are a trusted professional.

With every piece of content that you share...

❖ Social media posts
❖ Blog posts
❖ Emails
❖ Videos
❖ Inspirational graphics
❖ Meditations
❖ Affirmations
❖ Audiobooks
❖ Podcasts

...you will continue to establish yourself as an expert in your field. As someone who knows exactly what they're talking about.

When you consistently demonstrate to your ideal client the depth of your experience and knowledge, you are showing just how much value you are providing and that in your industry you are the leading authority.

The more expertise you display, the more confidence your audience will have in you and they will come to you to solve their problems.

The more value you share, the more it shows people that you know exactly what you're talking about and should be looked at as a trusted advisor.

Personal Unique Branding™ Allows You to Attract Your Ideal Client

Being known as an expert in your field brings unique benefits with it.

When you're known as the expert in your industry:

❖ It attracts your ideal client--the people who need your help the most.

❖ You get more referrals from others in your industry and related industries.

❖ You can charge a premium price--the kind of price that only an expert can charge.

Tony Robbins is a prime example of this. We have witnessed firsthand his UPW, Unleash the Power Within, events going from less than a thousand people in 1993 to over 15,000 today. For years, he has been sharing the same unique branded message of self-empowerment.

Everything he says, every video he puts out, every book he writes has the same brand message: You can develop into a powerful individual and I can help you to do that.

LISA LIEBERMAN-WANG & TONY ROBBINS

Over time, he has established himself as one of, if not *the*, go-to person in the self-development arena.

The results?

 ❖ He attracts huge audiences of people who want to fulfill their potential.
 ❖ Millions of people read his books, watch his videos and follow him on social media.
 ❖ He can charge a premium price for his services.

By consistently building his Personal Unique Brand™ over many years, Tony Robbins now has the world's most influential people flocking to him for advice.

Do you want to experience the Tony Robbins effect?

Not just observers of what Tony created, both Lisa and Willard studied and worked with him over the past two and a half.
 decades. Willard became a corporate facilitator for Robbins Research and Lisa progressed to be one of the elite few who hold the position of Trainer for Tony Robbins.

If you want to be known as the go-to person in your industry, then it's essential that you begin building your Personal Unique Brand™ as soon as possible.

Personal Unique Branding™ Puts You in Charge of the Narrative

As we noted earlier, your Personal Unique Brand™ will evolve, whether you want it to or not. If you:

- ❖ Use social media
- ❖ Have an email list
- ❖ Have a blog
- ❖ Speak to groups
- ❖ Record and share videos

...you are already creating your Personal Unique Brand™. Everything you project to the world is part of your Personal Unique Brand™.

The question is whether you intend to mold your brand's narrative or not.

In other words, do you figure out exactly what your brand is all about, or do you allow it to unfold in a haphazard way?

Is your brand being carefully curated or is your brand "evolving" on its own? Are you the one who influences the opinions of people about you, or are you just letting things happen?

The hidden, extraordinary strength of a strategic Personal Unique Brand™ approach is that it assures that your own narrative is consciously created.

Instead of just letting them form their own opinions, you influence what others think of you. You are now the master over how prospects perceive you, no longer powerless in the face of their own automatic assumptions or limiting beliefs that could otherwise shape their views of you.

You carefully construct everything you share, every blog post you write, every email you send, you tell the story of who you are. You are the author of your story.

Personal Unique Branding™

Increases Your Visibility

The more you build your Personal Unique Brand™, the more visible you'll become.

❖ You'll attract more fans on social media.
❖ Those fans will share your content with their tribes.
❖ The more your content gets shared, the more clients you'll attract.
❖ And repeat!

It's a powerful process. You can even expect to be featured in the media as your fan base grows. These are just a few we have been featured in already.

Media outlets are always searching for experts to discuss specific topics, and you will start generating media inquiries as you are recognized as the expert in your field. The more media outlets you're featured in, the more opportunities you're going to have to present your topic to crowds hungry for your message. Organizers of conferences are always seeking to book well-known media personalities.

The truth is, building your Personal Unique Brand™ and building your platform go hand-in-hand.

As your Personal Unique Brand™ grows stronger, your platform will get bigger, which will then make your brand stronger.

Building your brand is a fundamental strategy that brings greater and greater results the more you do it.

Personal Unique Branding™ Shapes What Content You Share

If you don't have a powerful Personal Unique Brand™, then you don't have any direction on what information to share with your audience. Without that clear direction, at any given moment you end up sharing either nothing or everything that catches your fancy. Neither one of those approaches adds to your Personal Unique Brand™.

This level of clarity points you to exactly what kinds of content you need to share when you have a solid Personal Unique Brand™.

Simply put, you will only share content that aligns with your Personal Unique Brand's™ values and reinforces them.

A video may be interesting, but you shouldn't share it if it doesn't add to your Personal Unique Brand™.

Be sure that when posting images, you use your logo. Develop a theme, colors and an image that you want to utilize to attract your ideal client. Always stay consistent with your brand.

Be sure that you research color psychology when choosing your palate to see how different colors affect perceptions and behaviors. Here are a few of ours that we use separately and together with different products or services.

Personal Unique Branding™ Connects You More with Your Ideal Client

The simple truth is that people are more connected to an individual than to a company. That's why Elon Musk, an engineer and technology entrepreneur designer of SpaceX and Richard Branson, business magnate, investor, author, philanthropist, founder of Virgin Group have more followers on Twitter than the businesses they created.

The more you work to build your Personal Unique Brand™, the more people will want to connect with you online and in-person. People will be drawn to your ideals, your personality, your opinions, and your perspectives.

The more connected you are, the more opportunities for doing business will come to you. You'll find yourself getting requests for even more speaking engagements. Further opportunities for media appearances. The ability to collaborate with other like-minded individuals.

Creating your Personal Unique Brand™ attracts potential customers and clients who will enthusiastically support your business.

With so many new businesses popping up online, a brand that links to a person's face is much easier for a potential client to trust. Compared to establishing a company brand, developing a relationship with a Personal Unique Brand™ takes less time and effort.

Personal Unique Branding™ Allows You to Become an Influencer

The more your Personal Unique Brand™ grows, the more you are recognized as an "influencer." An influencer is someone who tremendously shapes their followers' opinions and has a considerable impact on their behavior.

Being an influencer has some major benefits:

❖ Big brands want to work with influencers who have large audiences, which can result in more revenue for you.
❖ You often receive free things from companies who are interested in partnering with you.
❖ You receive media requests to speak at or even just attend events.

If you want to get in on these perks, start working to develop your Personal Unique Brand™.

"Influencers are "paid per post" and often develop long-term partnerships with well-known brands. You're able to network with millions of people and brands, many of which are of high caliber – allowing unlimited opportunities for joint ventures" according to Brit L'Amour @brit_lamour who became an influencer on Instagram.

Most influencers make an income of six figures purely from brand endorsements and paid partnerships.

The Power of a Personal Unique Brand™

Are you starting to see the power of your Personal Unique Brand™? Your Personal Unique Brand™ is what enables you to distinguish yourself from the competition. It allows you to charge a premium price for your services.

The more you concentrate on your Personal Unique Brand™, the more you become identifiable as the expert in your field. The more you are perceived to be an expert, the more opportunities you will have available to you.

And ultimately, the more you're establishing your Personal Unique Brand™, the more you're interacting with others, which in turn generates even more business and specifically more revenue.

Remember that people prefer connecting with people. It is now more important than ever to have a Personal Unique Brand™. If you are an entrepreneur in today's market, it is crucial that CEOs and company / brand owners come out of their offices and interact with their consumers.

It's safe to say that few things are stronger than your Personal Unique Brand™. The more you focus on developing it, the more you will see results.

Now, you ready to start building your Personal Unique Brand™.

BUILD YOUR PERSONAL BRAND

Chapter 3

How to Brand You

Now that you know why you need to be building a Personal Unique Brand™, let's talk about how. Let's break down several specific strategies for creating your own incredibly powerful Personal Unique Brand™.

Step #1:

Determine Who You Really Are

The first step in creating a powerful Personal Unique Brand™ is to determine who you are. Remember, building your Personal Unique Brand™ is about sharing your authentic self with the world. *

Branding doesn't mean you're being portrayed as something you're not. It's about consciously and creatively expressing your authentic self to your fans and clients. Your Personal Unique Brand™ should be a true reflection of your strengths, desires, values, and beliefs. It should also be a true reflection of your talents, passions ideals, and convictions.

In other words, your Personal Unique Brand™ is based on your skills, passions, values, and beliefs. If you want to build a strong Personal Unique Brand™, you need to know yourself.

We referred earlier to the **confidence formula** and the creation of your intellectual property.

Start by asking yourself:

- ❖ What unique skills do I have?
- ❖ What are my core values?
- ❖ What am I most passionate about?

* What unique experiences have shaped who I am?
* How can I most effectively serve my core audience?
* What do I have to offer that no one else does?

The answers to these questions should shape your Personal Unique Brand™. They should help you get to the core of what matters most to you and how you can add value to your audience.

Step #2:

Determine What You Want to Accomplish

Once you've identified the core of who you are, it's time to think about what you want to accomplish with your Personal Unique Brand™.

Answer these questions:

- ❖ What would I like to accomplish, both personally and professionally?
- ❖ What do I want to be known for?
- ❖ If I could be the world's foremost expert on a topic, what would it be?
- ❖ What key message do I want to communicate?
- ❖ If I could only give one piece of advice, what would it be?

The answers to these questions should further solidify in your mind what your Personal Unique Brand™ will look like.

Step #3:

Identify Your Ideal Client

The simple reality is that you are not able to serve everyone successfully. Instead, there's a core audience that will resonate strongly with you, your brand, and what you're offering.

This core demographic is your ideal client. It's these people you're going to serve most effectively and they're going to become your raving fans.

To identify your ideal client avatar, ask yourself these questions:

- ❖ Who can I most effectively help?
- ❖ Who will benefit most from my skill set and knowledge?
- ❖ Who am I most passionate about serving?
- ❖ Who will resonate most with me and my brand?

When determining your ideal client, it can be helpful to create a persona. This persona represents your ideal client.

Include the following information in the persona:

- ❖ Demographics: How old are they? Male? Female? Single? Married? What is their level of education? What career are they in? How much do they make?

❖ Hopes and dreams: What do they want their future to look like? What are their goals?

❖ Problems: What obstacles do they face? Why haven't they been able to reach their goals? What keeps them up at night?

The key to a great Personal Unique Brand™ is how well you understand your ideal client and their problems. Then, you can establish why you care and how you can solve these problems. This is what you will be recognized for: Solving their greatest problem.

Step #4:

Create Your Sensational

Soundbyte™

Now it's time to create your Sensational Soundbyte™.

Your Sensational Soundbyte™ is your brand summed up into a single, powerful compelling statement that describes exactly what you do for your audience and differentiates you from the competition.

It's where you take all the answers from the previous questions and put them together into one brand statement that sums up who you are personally and how you serve your ideal client.

A Sensational Soundbyte™ typically looks something like this:

Typically, I work with (Ideal Client) _____
Who have the challenge of (Problem) _____
I help them get (Advantages) _____
What that means is (Benefits) _____

Who do you know who might be interested in something like this? (CTA)

For example, your Sensational Soundbyte™ may be something like this **one promoting a program called the *Big Money Blueprint™*.**

"*Typically, we work with Coaches, Consultants & Entrepreneurs who have the challenge of trading time for money, not being seen as the expert, and increasing sales.*

We help them separate themselves from the competition and charge a premium for their services using the Big Money Blueprint™.

What that means is they can have certainty and peace of mind as their business grows exponentially and profitably.

Who do you know who might be interested in taking their business to the next level?"

Or, promoting the NAP Leadership & Coaching Academy™

"*Typically, we work with Professionals who have the challenge of wanting to transition into a career of helping more people but are concerned about how they will 1) get results for their clients and 2) replace their current income.*

We help them get the skills of the top 1% of coaches in the world, make personal transformations themselves and help them develop a 3-year strategic plan designed to create a 6-figure plus coaching business.

What that means is that they can live their lives focused on fulfilling their purpose, enjoying what they do each day impacting lives and have the security in knowing that their financial future is in their control.

Who do you know who might be interested in something like this?"

Or, promoting Anatomy of Transformation program

Typically, I work with people at a major turning point in their life.

They have the challenge of knowing that they have the potential to do and be more, but are constantly falling short of their goals or never getting started and losing hope of ever attaining their dreams.

I help them get clarity on what is really holding them back, get leverage to commit to what needs to be done and connect them with the resources that will lead their ultimate transformation.

What that means is they can finally have the certainty express themselves fully and connect with their greatest potential allowing them to truly transform their personal and professional life into the one they have always dreamed it could be.

Who do you know who might be interested in something like this?

Or, promoting F.I.N.E. to FAB™ a Personal Development program

"Typically, I work with successful individuals in some areas but not with themselves. They are hurting themselves and feeling "F.I.N.E.", which is how I used to feel, Frustrated, Insecure, Neurotic and Emotional .

I help them go from feeling F.I.NE. to being FAB, Fabulous, Awesome, Beautiful. What that means is they can avoid years of shame, blame and therapy™.

Who do you know who might be interested in something like this?"

Your Sensational Soundbyte™ doesn't have to tell everything about your brand, but it should get to the heart of who you are and how you serve your audience.

It may help to give a unique name to your Sensational Soundbyte™ that will be something that people remember. As an example, you might call your Sensational Soundbyte™ the "Small Business Success Secrets" if you teach people how to be more successful in business.
Or if you help entrepreneurs grow their sales, you could call your Sensational Soundbyte™ something like, "The Big Money Blueprint™."

You get the point. It simply needs to be short, memorable, and aptly describe what you do.

Avoid skimping on this step. Take the necessary time to craft a Sensational Soundbyte™ that adequately captures what your Personal Unique Brand™ is about.

Step #5:

Start Treating Yourself

as a Brand

Once you've identified the core of your brand, as well as your ideal client, it's time to start treating yourself as a brand.

What does this look like practically?

You need to remain true to your brand message in every conversation with your audience, whether it's a blog post, email, podcast, social media post, etc.

You are constantly talking about the problems you address, constantly inspiring your audience, constantly expressing the brand's message.

Just like Nike wouldn't start talking about camping unexpectedly, make sure that your communications don't detract from the brand. In everything you do, you are continuously reinforcing your Personal Unique Brand™.

It also means creating a powerful, engaging website that will serve as your home base for all of your online activities (more about this in a minute).

This means creating a publicity page or media kit for media inquiries on your website.

It might mean not answering emails yourself but answering them via an assistant (or answering them under a pseudonym). It depends on the brand you are looking to portray.

If you want to delegate some of the responsibility it should be things that don't require your voice.

Your outcome is to present yourself as an influential, powerful brand, not just a normal person. You must view yourself as you wish to be perceived: a powerful brand with a powerful message.

Step #6:

Optimize Your Website

Now it's time to get into the nitty-gritty of optimizing your online presence so that it matches your brand. You're going to start with your website, since this functions as your "home base" of sorts. In other words, your website is one of the primary places people get to know who you are and what you do.

Your website also serves as one of the quickest ways you transition visitors into paying clients. Make sure you invest in someone who knows what they are doing who will customize it for that specific purpose and do it correctly.

First impressions when it comes to your website are critical. Visitors should be able to instantly recognize how you can help solve their problems. If they can't see that immediately, they're going to leave and go somewhere else.

So, what do you need to do to make sure your site is communicating your brand?

❖ Have your website done professionally by someone who understand story brand marketing and SEO, search engine marketing. If you want to hire a company that knows this process go to YLW Consulting Services.

❖ Have a professional logo designed. Having a professional logo shows people that you're serious about what you do and really do treat yourself as a brand. If you wish to hire someone to design a logo for you, 99 Designs, Fiverr and Upwork are great places to start.

❖ Show off your Sensational Soundbyte™. From the moment they arrive on your website, visitors should see your Sensational Soundbyte™. It's what will draw them in and make them want to investigate more.

❖ Ideally, your Sensational Soundbyte™ will be front and center at the top of your website so that it's likely to be the first thing that people see and impossible to miss. Let it function like the main headline on a newspaper and have their eye drawn to it immediately.

❖ Use professional photographs. Have a professional photographer take high-quality photos of you. Low-quality photos will ultimately reflect poorly on your brand. Purchase royalty free photos if necessary.

❖ Use testimonials. Testimonials are proof that you really can solve people's problems. They help overcome your prospects' resistance and objections. Also, if you've been featured in any media outlets, show off those credentials too.

❖ Present a clear call-to-action. Ultimately, you want people to take action when they're on your website. You want them to join your email list, watch your webinar, or sign up for a free consultation. Give visitors a clear path to connect with you and ask for the particular help or information they need now.

❖ Create a compelling "About" page. On your about, tell your story. How did you get to where you currently are? What motivates you to serve your audience? Why do you do what you do?

❖ Create a service page. If you want clients to hire you, it's important to have a clear services page in which you explain what you offer, what's included, and more.

❖ Give away free resources. One of the best ways to build your brand is to give away free content on your website. This could be anything from blog posts to videos to an ebook.

Giving away content in exchange for a visitor's email address is also a fantastic way to grow your email list.

❖ Create a contact page. Obviously, you want a way for people to be in touch with you. This will happen primarily through your contact page on your website.

Step #7:

Develop Your Content Strategy

The primary way to build your brand is by creating strategic content. By content, we mean blog posts, videos, social media posts, emails, affirmations, podcasts, and more.

Whatever content you share with your audience should be used to establish your brand. As we mentioned earlier, it's important to start treating yourself as a brand once you've defined your brand.

Developing a strategic content strategy is one of the most powerful ways to make sure your messaging always remains focused on the brand.

When it comes to your content strategy, we recommend the "Pillar Method" (a term coined by Gary Vaynerchuk).

The Pillar Method works as follows:

❖ At set intervals (every day, every week, etc.) create a longer piece of "pillar" content. This could be a blog post, video, ebook, etc. The point is that it needs to be on the longer side so that it can be repurposed in numerous ways.

❖ This pillar content should always reinforce some part of your brand. Maybe one day you speak to a particular pain point. Another day you encourage your audience to strive for their goals. Whatever the case, it's essential that your pillar content always be tied back to your brand.

❖ Publish your pillar content on your primary platform, whether that's your blog, YouTube, iTunes, etc.

❖ Take your pillar content and cut it up into smaller, shareable pieces of content. In other words, if you have a 10-minute video, find three parts of that video that could be shared on their own and extract those clips.

❖ If you have a 1,000-word blog post, extract five 100-word excerpts that can stand on their own. Repurpose everything.

❖ Share the smaller pieces of content across all your channels. Once you've created your smaller pieces of content, you're going to post those across all your channels, including Facebook, Instagram, LinkedIn, Twitter, email, etc.

❖ If the thought of posting to so many social media channels intimidates you, Buffer is a great tool that allows you to share to all your social media at one time. You just put the content in and then select all the channels you want it to go out to. Or you can hire a virtual assistant on Upwork to do it for you.

❖ Repeat the process again and again. Consistency is the key. By consistently sharing your brand message, you'll steadily build your audience.

By using the "Pillar Method" for your content strategy, you ensure that every piece of content you post is always on brand. Your Facebook posts, Instagram videos, blog posts, YouTube videos, LinkedIn and emails always are speaking your brand message to your audience.

In addition to using the "Pillar Method", you can also simply repurpose content into different formats. For example, you can turn an ebook into a SlideShare presentation or a series of blog posts into an ebook. Or you could turn a blog post into an email you send out to your list.

The main point is that everything you send out should be brand related. You want to constantly reinforce your brand to your audience.

Step #8:

Constantly Add Value to Your Audience

It is extremely important that you constantly give value to your audience when it comes to building your brand, without asking for anything in return. Yes, there are moments when you are inviting people to buy from you or become a client, but you don't want that to be your brand's main theme.

When interacting with your brand, the main thing people should take away is how much value you continually provide.

Your main way of adding value is through your content strategy. That's why the frequent release of new content is so critical.

If you're not putting out new content, you're not giving away value.

A great Personal Unique Brand™ is one with a high impact level, which leads to success amongst the people who follow you. The aim is to use social media and other social platforms and communities in order to create substantive and important conversations between you and the people you want to influence.

Step #9:

Build a Community

One of the best ways to build your brand is to build a community where everyone can help each other. The value of building a community around your brand is that it inspires others to help promote your brand.

You create a tribe of passionate people who care about the same things you do.
So how can you build a community?

Some simple ways to build a community include:

❖ Start a private Facebook group. In this group, people can interact with each other, share ideas, interact with you, raise questions, etc.

❖ Host live events. Live events allow you to meet members of your tribe in person. Coffee meetups, retreats, workshops, masterminds, and private dinners are all great ways to deepen your relationships with them.

❖ Create a membership site. For a small monthly fee, you can give people exclusive access to you and the content you provide. You can also give them access to things like group calls every month, ongoing webinars, and a forum where they can interact with you and other members.

Now Is the Time to Brand You

The simple truth is, if you want to or not, you have a Personal Unique Brand™. Everything you share with your audience will either add or take away the value from your Personal Unique Brand™. You must be absolutely committed to building your brand.

We all have a Personal Unique Brand™ regardless of whether we think so or not. So, choose to be strategic about developing it.

Luckily, building a Personal Unique Brand™ is not difficult.

Here's a quick summary of what we covered:

- ❖ Identify what matters to you.
- ❖ Define your ideal client.
- ❖ Create your Sensational Soundbyte™.
- ❖ Treat yourself like a brand.
- ❖ Create your compelling website.
- ❖ Create your content strategy.
- ❖ Constantly bring your best self to your audience.

❖ Build your community.

The more you do those things, the more you'll build your brand and the more you'll attract an audience of raving fans.

Avoid waiting any longer to build your Personal Unique Brand™. Get started on it today! Your audience needs you. Get out there and start serving them. You'll be glad you did!

*Limited Bonus Offer

Request a FREE Consultation to see if and how we can support you in growing your business.

Lisa Lieberman-Wang and Willard Barth invite you or a friend to apply for a private discovery call.

Apply Now:

www.BrandYouBecomeTheExpert.com/Apply

*The offer is open to all purchasers of BRAND YOU BECOME THE EXPERT by Lisa Lieberman-Wang & Willard Barth. The offer is limited to qualified individuals and availability of time in the schedule as deemed by Superlative Alternatives, Inc. Superlative Alternatives, Inc reserves the right to refuse consultation to anyone it believes does not qualify. This is a limited time offer. The value of this FREE consultation for you or a friend is $750 as of time printed. Participant in the consultations are under no additional financial obligation whatsoever to Superlative Alternatives, Inc. Free consultation not redeemable for cash.

Limited Bonus Offer

Limited to speakers, coaches, consultants, business owners and entrepreneurs looking to take themselves and their business to the next level.

We are working privately with a small group of individuals who are ready to invest in themselves.

If you qualify let us help you make a difference, get your message out to the world, grow your business and increase your revenue now.

Simply apply for a free consultation. Fill out the form and let's see how we can help you.

We find people get this far and drop the ball ... 90% will never follow through. So, if you are interested, fill out the request right now, and give us as much information as you can.

Because this is a customized program, we're only offering this to a limited few who qualify. So, if you are serious about investing in yourself and growing your business, **take action now**.

We look forward to hearing from you. This is something we usually charge for, and we are offering this as a one-time opportunity. We would love to give you the resources to make a difference and help others also grown and change for the better.

To apply go to:

www.BrandYouBecomeTheExpert.com/Apply

Lisa Lieberman-Wang

Speaker, Trainer, Business & Life Strategist

Lisa Lieberman-Wang is the #1 Best Seller of FINE to FAB and a leading expert on neuroscience and human psychology. Co-Creator of the cutting-edge neuroscience N.A.P., Neuro Associative Programming™ (NAP), she is a Licensed Master NLP Practitioner and Trainer.

Lisa is a sought-after keynote speaker for 25 years, addressing over 125,000 people in person in the U.S. and worldwide on leadership, mindset, sales and marketing, and how to grow themselves and their businesses.

Lisa has been seen by millions on ABC, NBC, CBS, FOX, and the CW as their Business & Life Strategist. She has spoken on some of the most prestigious stages, including TEDx, Harvard University, the Navy, Carnegie Hall. Most recently,  she has also been recognized as one of the Top 25 Leading Women Entrepreneurs.

Lisa helps you become even more successful personally and professionally by removing the blocks that get in your way of true happiness while giving you proven tools and strategies to build a purposeful life and profitable business. She supports professionals and corporations to up-level themselves and their businesses.

She has done over $60 million in personal sales in her prior corporate career. She has led countless professionals to multi-million-dollar businesses including herself.

She took one company's sales team from 7% closing ratios to 91% in a few hours equating to hundreds of thousands in new revenue in one year and millions over lifetime value of the client. She has helped businesses owners and executives double, triple and 10x their revenue. Lisa's expertise reaches and transforms every aspect of your business.

For more information about booking Lisa, visit her website or call **1-877-250-7275** today.

Contact Info
www.LisaLiebermanWang.com
www.FINEtoFAB.com
www.NAPCoachingAcademy.com
Email: Lisa@FINEtoFAB.com

Willard Barth

Speaker, Trainer, Executive Business Strategist

Willard Barth is an Executive Business Strategist with over 22 years of creating extraordinary success for his clients. What he has discovered is that from small startups to multi-national corporations, for a business to be successful they all follow a repetitive cycle that he labels "The Anatomy Of Transformation".

#1 Best Selling Author, International Speaker, Co-Creator of the cutting-edge neuroscience N.A.P., Neuro Associative Programming™ (NAP), Business Consultant, Coach and Trainer.

Willard has gone from a life of total devastation to being one of the leading consultants in his field. How? That's what you will learn when you hear his presentation.

His system and book "The Anatomy of Transformation" is the result of the more than 30 years that he has spent working with and observing tens of thousands of individuals and hundreds of companies.

One company using this system increased their sales by 93% in one year. Another corporation that Willard's team is working with became one of the 10 fastest growing companies in NJ for 2014, and one of the 2,000 fastest growing companies in the United States.

Willard is known for getting clients explosive results in both their professional and personal lives. companies and thousands of people to get them explosive results in both their professional and personal lives. His presentations are humorous, entertaining, powerful and include strategies and techniques that empower the participants to get instant results.

For more information about booking Willard, visit his website or call **570-279-7620** today.

Contact Info
www.WillardBarth.com
www.NAPCoachingAcademy.com
Email: Willard@willardbarth.com

Brand You Become the Expert
Demonstration & Implementation

Now we will share two of our successful programs that we created based on the very principles explained in this book. They are currently serving thousands of clients and generating millions in revenue – for ourselves and our clients who have been educated in this proven methodology.

Big Money Blueprint™ and NAP Leadership & Coaching Academy™ have been changing lives and helping to build businesses of individuals just like you. Using cutting edge neuroscience, psychology, time tested and proven methodologies we help you break through the noise and guide you to take your gifts and share them with the world in a way they can and will be heard by your ideal client.

No longer is your Personal Unique Brand™ the best kept secret once you have **BRANDED YOURSELF AS THE EXPERT!**

Big Money Blueprint™

The "Big Money Blueprint™" is a comprehensive, proven, 6-week program specifically for speakers, coaches, consultants and business owners designed to give them the "edge" that will set themselves apart from the competition.

We will share a proven formula with you giving you everything you need to know to help grow your business fast and improve the results you're getting with your clients even more!

Our system is designed to guide you step by step in creating your own brand identity, a signature program/service that you will become known for, a signature talk designed to easily convert prospects into clients... no more fear or struggle in selling... and designing a step by step process to maximize results for you, your clients AND increase profits.

Facilitated by Certified Master Trainers

Lisa Lieberman-Wang and Willard Barth

During the class, you will be guided by us to create:

THE FOUNDATION

❖ **Develop Your Confidence Formula™** This is what truly differentiates you from the competition. During this process you will identify the key benefits your client will get from working with you and why you are the ONLY person qualified to work with them!

❖ **Create your Personal IP** (Intellectual Property) This is an incredible introspective process that helps you realize the "What, Why and How" that is uniquely YOU and becomes the foundation for the program you will become known for, making you THE Expert in your field.

❖ **Identify your Ideal Client Avatar** There is a very specific person who wants, needs and can afford your services. We help you create a very specific avatar... so specific you can speak directly to their biggest problem and greatest pain and let them know that you have a proven formula to help them overcome it.

❖ **The NAP Sensational Soundbyte™** How to

communicate what you do and for whom effectively and succinctly - We'll teach you the right formula to share with people what you do, who you do it for, what problems you will solve and the benefits to them.

❖ **Optimize Client Acquisition** We show you how to tie everything you've created above to get the best ROI on your marketing efforts and attract the RIGHT clients for your product or service.

YOUR PERSONALIZED PROGRAM OR SERVICE

o **Creating YOUR Proven Formula for Results**
Realize that people do not buy a product or service. They buy a result. We will guide you to identify your own step by step process that will take your client from where they are to where they desire to go.

o **Structuring the RIGHT Pricing**
Understanding the value of your time and the impact you will make is key to helping you grow a profitable business AND finding clients who will truly commit to the process. We help you to discover that value and set

your pricing accordingly.

❖ **Create Funnels to Attract Ideal Client-** Learn how to attract, collect and nurture online/offline your ideal client. We teach you the formula for developing and filling your funnel with the right prospects.

❖ **Maximize Your Funnel** - In this next step, you need to convert the ideal prospects captured above into a client and then a raving fan. Learn the Low Hanging Fruit strategy to educate and convert; then automate for efficiency and enhanced service delivery/relationship.

❖ **Strategic Online and Offline Marketing** - If you're marketing to everyone, you're selling to no one. Create your specific strategy to attract more of the your ideal client to your product or service.

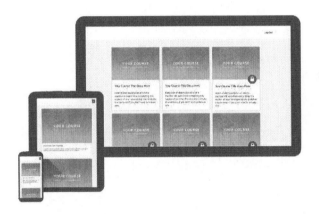

❖ **Creating Your NAP Signature Talk™ - This is** the introduction to your Signature Program. You will learn to create your presentation using a proven formula to help your prospect realize if your product service is right for them and get them to take action **now.**

❖ **YOUR Signature Program**   This is your customized program that solves the problem/pain that your Ideal Client is facing.

Did you know that businesses that struggle tend to sell *hours?* Successful businesses are known for being able to help their client get a specific *outcome*. That outcome is sold not as time but as a program or package with a defined path to the result.

❖ **Choosing the Right Name for Your Signature Program and Signature Talk** People are buying the result, not the formula for getting it. Learn how to use your Ideal Client's own language to create a title that captures their attention and gets them excited to invest in your product or service.

❖ **The SmartNAP Close™** Learn the powerful "Interview-Takeaway" and "Discovery" methods to "close the sale" *without* coming across like a pushy salesperson. This is the win/win secret to selling high ticket items.

EXECUTION AND ENSURING YOUR CLIENTS GET AMAZING RESULTS

❖ **Use Technology to Your Advantage You will be taught** a step-by-step guide for creating lead capture and online delivery of your Signature Talk. You will learn how to implement technology to automate as much of the process as possible, leaving more time for you to focus on doing what you love and do best!

❖ **Create the Most Efficient Step-by-Step Process for Delivering Your Signature Program** Your Signature program/service will be a process that walks your clients through their own process. It can be 1:1, group, self-study, live retreats or a combination of them all. You'll learn to create a process that you can use again and again that gives the client a consistent path to success.

❖ **Learn what Technology is Best Suited to Deliver Your Signature Program** There are plenty of options based on what your program/service delivers as well as your budget.

❖ **Create Raving Fans** Learn how to engage your client in an ongoing process to ensure that they get extraordinary results and become a referral mechanism for your business.

AND you also get...

❖ Access to the secure membership site

❖ Weekly video training modules

❖ Written documentation to support the video training

- ❖ A robust Online Resource section
- ❖ Interactive support from Lisa Lieberman-Wang and Willard Barth via text and email to help you in executing what you are learning
- ❖ Group discussions with your classmates
- ❖ Weekly LIVE group coaching interactive sessions facilitated by Lisa and Willard

If you are interested in learning more about Big Money Blueprint,™

Apply for a Complimentary Call today:
www.BrandYouBecomeTheExpert.com/Apply

LEADERSHIP & COACHING ACADEMY
Changing Lives Through The Art Of Neuroscience

Are You Interested in Mastering Leadership and Communication Skills to Create Even More Transformation with Others?

Join Lisa and Willard in their 12-month Certification Program: N.A.P. Leadership & Coaching Academy™!

One of the key components in being a leader today is your ability to draw the very best out of the people around you. You become not only a leader, but also a mentor, consultant and coach. To help someone reach their fullest potential you need to become a master of understanding human behavior. The only way to influence someone is by learning, understanding and applying what already influences them.

We are programmed at an early age to believe what is right and wrong, good or bad, what we are capable of and what we aren't, what to do or not do. At one point in our lives these programs may have served us, but in time

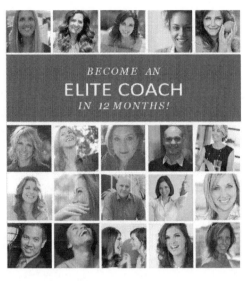

these programs can become antiquated and need to be decompiled because they are no longer having the desired result. But even if you knew how to decompile or change the old programs you will still need to install new upgrades.

The human mind is very similar to a computer and these programs are your automated systems for living. They determine all the little things you do every day that impact your quality of life. Some people are running programs that make daily living so challenging that they need an entirely new operating system. Think of it like this, if we were using a computer running on

DOS today, we would not be on the internet, we needed to upgrade to Windows. As our environment and needs change, we need to be using new programs to help us operate at our greatest potential.

It has been said that the human brain is the most powerful supercomputer on the planet. Based on that premise, if we can program computers to do what people do then we can also program unresourceful individuals to do what successful ones are doing.

To achieve this level of transformation with someone the idea of just getting a "life coach" is not going to work. In order to truly reach this level of optimum performance in your life the world needs a new kind of coach, one that takes into account the whole person, mind, body and spirit. One that understands the art of neuroscience and how we are programmed. We call this new kind of professional a Certified NAP & NLP Practitioner. These are people who have gone through intense training to understand and use the keys to unlocking true potential and happiness in their clients.

Our curriculum begins the road to mastery as a Certified Neuro Associative Programming (N.A.P.) & Neuro-Linguistic Programming (N.L.P.) Practitioner bringing together cutting edge neuroscience, psychology, therapy, intuitive listening, results focused coaching with proven skills and techniques to update the operating system and eliminate programs that no longer serve your clients which allow them to install new upgrades that create optimum performance.

❖ Founded by Lisa Lieberman-Wang and Willard Barth, N.A.P. Coaching, this in-depth twelve-month program is recognized as the most comprehensive in the industry which utilizes technology based training, group sessions, hands-on coaching, ongoing group work, mentoring from Master Trainers and two intimate LIVE weekend immersion seminars. At the completion of this one-year certification program you will be eligible to become a Certified NAP & NLP Practitioner.

❖ 80% of the course is taught online. This gives you the ability to learn from anywhere in the world. It also allows you to do the majority of the coursework around your schedule.

❖ New graduates who have decided to make a career as a N.A.P. and NLP Practitioner have earned as much as $21,000 in 10 days (that was before even graduating from the course). By the end of the month, that N.A.P. and NLP Practitioner had generated over $45,000!

❖ There are no prerequisites. Anyone passionate about making a difference and helping people can benefit from this course. We have helped business owners grow their businesses, improve sales and lead their teams more effectively. And we have had students who have launched successful coaching practices, run group programs, retreats and more!

❖ Gain the skill set of the top 1% of influencers in the world in 12 months!

Why N.A.P. Leadership & Coaching Academy™?

N.A.P. Leadership & Coaching Academy™ is revolutionizing leadership, influence and professional coaching by teaching components of neuroscience, psychology and therapy to our students giving them the best resources available. This in-depth twelve-month program utilizes online, offline, real-time, free time, and in person scenarios.

As a leading, global coaching organization, it's our commitment to help maximize your potential through life coaching, professional coaching, and personal coaching as ways of enriching your lives and creating better and more profitable opportunities. Our specialized coaching programs, courses, and workshops are designed to create positive change, regardless of the types of goals. We aim to inspire and to radically change the way you invest your time and energy for the better.

How Do I Become a Certified N.A.P. & N.L.P. Practitioner?

The Certification Program begins the road to mastery as a N.A.P. & N.L.P. Practitioner. This in-depth twelve-month program includes utilizing technology-based training, group sessions hands-on coaching, ongoing group work and two LIVE 3-day weekend immersion seminars. At the completion of this one-year certification program you will be eligible to take the written and oral certification exam, with the goal of becoming a Certified N.A.P. & N.L.P. Practitioner.

What is N.A.P.?

Created by Lisa Lieberman-Wang and Willard Barth, Neuro-Associative Programming is the culmination of years of research and application of proven principles of neuroscience relating to how human beings take in, sort, store, access and utilize information and experiences. What that means to you is that you will begin to understand these beneath-the-surface human processes. As a N.A.P. practitioner, you will learn how you can use very specific protocols to reprogram how this information is stored, accessed and used. By adjusting the programming, you change the level of potential an individual can access.

What Distinguishes N.A.P. Leadership & Coaching Academy™?

❖ Specialized N.A.P. Training Programs in addition

to business and marketing skills refinement to help you become even more successful.

❖ N.A.P. Coaching Academy online learning system lets you learn with convenience wherever you are, while participating in live, interactive, engaged training and practice.

❖ Your two LIVE Weekend Intensives help you expand your skills during interactive exercises exponentially.

❖ Coach and Be Coached. Learn not only how to coach but put your learning into practice. Talk the talk and walk the walk outside the traditional classroom or conference room.

❖ Small, intimate class size affords much personal attention and opportunity to practice so that the student can become a great N.A.P. Practitioner.

❖ Our faculty is second to none in passion and real-world neuroscience, psychology, therapy and coaching business building experience.

N.A.P. Leadership & Coaching Academy™ Course Curriculum

N.A.P. Leadership & Coaching Academy's™ curriculum has taken the best of understanding centuries of human psychology to give you the necessary tools to help facilitate change in individuals quickly and easily. We took over fifty years of practical experience of the founders, working with individuals in professional coaching utilizing neuroscience, psychology, cognitive behavior therapy and more. We then did something *no other program offers*: We help you develop a 3-year business plan to achieve the success you desire doing what you love, helping others.

This is an in-depth twelve-month program utilizing online, offline, real-time, free time, in person scenarios. Our specialized coaching programs, courses, and workshops are designed to create positive change, whatever your aspirations are. We aim to inspire you and to radically change the way you make change in individuals for the better and enhance the quality of your life doing it.

If you are interested in learning more about NAP Leadership & Coaching Academy™ visit www.NAPCoachingAcademy.com

Apply for a Complimentary Call at:
www.NAPCoachingAcademy.com/Apply

BRAND YOU

BECOME THE EXPERT

Summation

Thank you for giving us the privilege to share with you how we have successfully implemented what you have just learned in **BRAND YOU BECOME THE EXPERT.** Now you can be among the thousands we have already instructed in creating their own **PERSONAL UNIQUE BRAND™.**

We look forward to hearing about your success as you apply these principles in your own business.

Please reach out to explore how we may assist you even more to successfully build more sales, to more clients, more often.

www.BRANDYOUBECOMETHEEXPERT.COM

Made in the USA
Columbia, SC
06 February 2020